British Railway Pict(

First Generation DMUs

Kevin Robertson

Ian Allan
PUBLISHING

First published 2004

ISBN 0 7110 2970 9

© Ian Allan Publishing Ltd 2004

Published by Ian Allan Publishing

an imprint of Ian Allan Publishing Ltd, Hersham, Surrey KT12 4RG.
Printed by Ian Allan Printing Ltd, Hersham, Surrey KT12 4RG.

Code: 0404/B1

Title page: **It is now half a century since the first of a batch of eight two-car DMUs built at the BR Derby Works entered service on Leeds-Bradford local services. With a body length of 57ft 6in and weighing 26–27 tons — depending on whether it was a DMC or DMBS — they were truly 'lightweight' vehicles. Unfortunately, tradition apparently dictated they would be fitted with a Leyland diesel engine developed for the LMSR in 1938, which was already outmoded. Even so, the sets performed useful work and were renowned for vibrating themselves and their passengers reasonably successfully for a 10-year period. All were withdrawn in early 1964.** *BR*

INTRODUCTION

Looking back now, it is hard to believe that nearly half a century has passed since the British Railways (BR) Modernisation Plan was published in 1955. I feel sure I am not alone in sometimes thinking back to what it must have been like on Britain's railways 50 years prior to that date. This was the time of Edwardian finery and a lifestyle which it is now only possible to experience through fading images and the interpretations of films or documentary makers who no doubt put their own slant on the finished result they wish us to see.

In 1905 or thereabouts, it would have been impossible to visualise how society and the subject in question, the railway system, would have changed by the mid-1950s, just as in 1955 it would have been difficult to imagine what the railways would be like at the beginning of the 21st century!

But what of the diesel multiple-unit (DMU) age? This was an era born as a result of the 1955 modernisation programme and one which promised to revolutionise rail travel in a way passengers may have sampled only briefly before. This method of rail transport was first experienced in Britain with steam-railmotors on various railways and with the Great Western Railway's (GWR) fleet of AEC diesel units, interspersed in time with 'one-offs', including the Michelin Pneumatic car, the GWR's petrol railcar, the London, Midland & Scottish (LMS) Railway's three-car diesel unit, and the

like. Things had been different in Ireland, however, with DMUs in regular service from the 1930s.

The DMU was born out of a need to radically change the method of train operation on the railway system. That this was a success is beyond question, and one only has to look at the very few passenger services which remain locomotive hauled today to understand the tremendous change the principle of multiple-unit operation has wrought. I do not forget, either, the contribution made by the widespread use of electric multiple-units (EMUs), although at the present time, extension of such services generally appears less likely than was at one time envisaged, and large numbers of new trains being produced today are still DMUs, albeit with electric or hydraulic transmission.

Consider, though, the difficulties facing the British Railways management in 1955 — a period even then when years of underinvestment and overuse were major concerns. Ever-increasing competition from other forms of transport, difficulties in recruiting staff, and falling revenue in areas where once there had been a monopoly, all exacerbated the problem.

Small wonder, then, that given what was almost a free-hand to spend, spend, spend, BR's Marylebone Road HQ was keen to develop the multiple-unit programme as quickly as possible. It hoped this would act as a saviour in stemming falling passenger traffic receipts and, as such, it was an opportunity to be grasped without delay.

CONTENTS

Right: **A development of the original Swindon Inter City units were the three- and six-coach Class 126 sets built at Swindon in 1959 and which were intended for the Scottish Region to augment the earlier fleet. In what was then its home area, a three-car set passes the site of the former Gollanfield station on 28 June 1966, forming the 2.30pm Inverness to Aberdeen express service. Beyond the train lie the waters of the Moray Firth and also the hills of the Black Isle.** *J. M. Boyes*

Taking into account the railway situation of the period as a whole, DMU operation was only a small part of modernising the network and there was a vast fleet of diesel locomotives to be ordered and introduced to replace main line steam, while additionally, route upgrades, electrification of the London Midland Region (LMR) main line, signalling improvements and freight handling were all major considerations.

Not surprisingly, BR had of necessity to turn to outside builders as well as using its own resources to produce a sufficient number of vehicles quickly enough, and in a story that mirrored the introduction of the main line and shunter diesel fleets, there were to be remarkable successes, and some appalling failures.

With hindsight it is easy to see why various avenues were considered: mechanical versus hydraulic transmission; aluminium against steel bodywork; corridor connections or not between sets and units. Unfortunately, it was also often a question of ordering straight off the drawing board without having any time to evaluate a single production unit in service. Trial running of an empty set was hardly likely to replicate the exacting demands of a full load going in or out of London, Manchester or Birmingham on an evening commuter service.

The DMU fleet was initially developed piecemeal, although by the early 1960s standardisation had emerged, with 'Blue Square' coupling compatability and mechanical transmission clearly the favoured option for all regions except the Southern. Such difficulties as did exist with unreliable performers were often offset by the displacement of sets by those rendered redundant elsewhere as branch line closures occurred.

Among early casualties were the small, four-wheeled diesel railbuses — 'too little and too late' could be said to be the epitaph here, although if they had not been tried at the time, no one would have known whether they would have been successful or not.

Aside from the introduction of the units themselves there was also the infrastructure in the form of new or rebuilt servicing facilities which were needed, as well as staff to be trained to operate and maintain the sets. In the latter category this represented further loss of the artisan grades resulting in the decline of steam locomotive maintenance, which could but only gather pace.

Generally, the new trains were well received by staff and public alike. Drivers preferred the clean working conditions and comfortable cabs, although one regular criticism was the presence of draughts, something they would have accepted without question in steam days!

Passengers too appreciated the light and airy accommodation, and the introduction of DMUs generally led to an increase in passenger numbers. However, the

presence of so much Formica and vinyl was an invitation to the vandal, and on evening and late night services one can understand the reluctance of a guard to remonstrate with a group of rowdy and perhaps drunken passengers. The driver too could suffer in this way; no longer in a separate vehicle to his passengers he was, on occasions, a tempting target.

The introduction of DMUs as an integrated unit carrying passengers and light goods in the same vehicle could be less than desirable. One example was the difficulties concerning the smell of fish when carried in the brake compartment on Norwich–Wells-next-the-Sea services.

One criticism levelled against the introduction of multiple-units, somewhat unfairly, was that all this change was really five to ten years too late. Perhaps there may be some justification in such a comment, but with the public purse having to fund innumerable other expensive projects in the same period following World War 2, all no doubt as or perhaps even more deserving, at least something was at last being done.

The long-term aim was of course for eventual wholesale electrification of the national network. Perhaps a further modernisation plan, in 1970 or '75, should have been made, but it was not to be and the major refurbishment programme of the 1970s indicated that the majority of the DMU fleet was still intended to continue in service for some years to come.

With a new generation of enthusiasts, to whom other forms of motive power were but a historic anachronism, it is perhaps of little surprise that there should be increasing interest in what has become known as the 'heritage fleet'. Slowly then, but gathering pace, the enthusiast would find the DMU sets of fascination, their often gently swaying motion allied to screaming engines and clunking gear changes, together with unparalleled views from the front and rear seats, a welcome relief from the swish electric efficiency seen elsewhere.

The exception, of course, was the Southern Region's diesel-electric multiple-units (DEMUs). Here, the familiarity was with the suburban electric stock, some passengers approving and some loathing them as they thumped their way along main lines and branches, always it seemed at the same sedate pace, a soporific experience that has led to more than one traveller finding himself carried some distance past his intended destination.

Back in 1955, any future successor to the then newly introduced DMUs would only have been seen as perhaps newer-designed units — but fashion dictates, and changing transport patterns and varying operating arrangements have often meant a later replacement has been designed to suit a different need. Such was the case when replacements were eventually considered in the 1980s with the introduction of 'second-generation' 'Sprinter' and 'Pacer' units.

The introduction of the new can result in the previous model becoming staid in appearance, and certainly 'heritage' units which survive into the present century can clearly be seen as belonging to a different era to today's 'Voyager' and 'Adelante'

fleets. As recounted above, it is an era which many enthusiasts will have witnessed, and like them or not, the first-generation-built units played their part, unsung for most of their lives, but responsible for moving countless millions in a regular and reliable way. They were the transition from the past to the present, and so fully justify the following they now have. Many of them are finding a new lease of life on Britain's heritage railways.

In producing this work I have taken the title in its literal sense and restricted the images used to that of DMUs in their pre-Rail Blue livery, introduced during the 1960s, wherever possible. In so doing, the illustrations represent the heyday of the type, and this is surely the aspect one would wish to convey.

I have drawn heavily on the work of two distinguished authors whose respective reference books on the subject have proved invaluable. For more information the reader is referred to: *British Rail DMUs & Diesel Railcars — Origins and First Generation Stock*, by Brian Morrison (Ian Allan Publishing), and *A Pictorial Record of British Railways Diesel Multiple-units* by Geoff Golding, published by the late Geoff Gamble under his Cheona imprint. For the first time, this latter book enabled a series of accurate drawings of DMUs to be made available. Sadly, at the time of writing, both these works were out of print. Other useful books consulted on the subject are: *British Rail Fleet Survey 8: Diesel Multiple-Units — The First Generation* by Brian Haresnape (Ian Allan Publishing); *British Multiple-Units Volume 1: DMUs and DEMUs* by Ashley Butlin; *The British Railcar: AEC to HST* by R. M. Tufnell (David & Charles) and *The Development of the Railcar* by R. W. Kidner (Oakwood).

Kevin Robertson
January 2004

Left: **A Cravens-build DMCL with four-digit roof indicator box, identified in the number series M51756-80. Designated Class 113, these units had hydraulic transmission which was hardly suitable for the task some were given, namely suburban work between St Pancras and Bedford. Most spent their entire lives based at Accrington on similar work in the Colne Valley in Lancashire. The difficulty was simply that the fluid transmission would overheat on what was essentially short hop working and accordingly they were all withdrawn by 1969.** *IAL*

DIESEL MULTIPLE-UNITS NUMBER SERIES

The table shows the multiple-unit number series as in use for 1968, the year of the greatest number of DMUs in service. Class numbers were not introduced until later but are included for additional information. Note that the regional prefixes have not been included within the number series but shown under regions allocated within the table.

The general pattern of DMU vehicle numbering was as follows:
79xxx for early units and four-wheel railbuses
50xxx for Driving Motor vehicles
55xxx for single-vehicle units
56xxx for Driving Trailer vehicles
59xxx for non-Driving Trailers (centre cars)
78xxx for the half-engined set vehicles converted 1982.
Note: In 1983 units in the 50xxx and 56xxx series were renumbered into the 53xxx and 54xxx series respectively to avoid duplication of identities with locomotives under TOPS.

No series	Built	Type	Class	Regions Allocated	Notes
50000-049	Derby	DMBS	114	E	2-car units
50050-091	Derby	DMBS	116	M/W	Suburban 3-car
50092-133	Derby	DMS	116	M/W	Suburban 3-car
50134-137	Met-Cam	DMBS	111	E	2-car units
50138-151	Met-Cam	DMC	101	E	4-car units
50152-157	Met-Cam	DMBS	101	E	2-car units
50158-163	Met-Cam	DMC(L)	101	E	2-car units
50164-167	Met-Cam	DMBS	101	E	2-car units
50168-171	Met-Cam	DMC(L)	101	E	2-car units
50172-197	Met-Cam	DMC	101	E	4-car units
50198-233	Met-Cam	DMBS	101	M	2-car units
50234-245	Met-Cam	DMC(L)	101	E	4-car units
50246-248	Met-Cam	DMBS	101	E	2-car units
50249	Cravens	DMBS	105	E	4-car unit
50250-259	Met-Cam	DMBS	101	E	2-car units
50260-269	Met-Cam	DMC(L)	101	E	2-car units
50270-279	Met-Cam	DMC(L)	111	E	3-car units
50280-292	Met-Cam	DMBS	111	E	3-car units
50293-296	Met-Cam	DMBS	101	M	2-car units
50303-320	Met-Cam	DMBS	101	M	3-car units
50321-338	Met-Cam	DMC(L)	101	M	3-car units
50339-358	Gloucester	DMBS	100	M/Sc	2-car units
50359-370	Cravens	DMBS	106	E	2-car units
50371-394	Cravens	DMBS	105	E	2-car units
50395-414	Park Royal	DMBS	103	M	2-car units
50415-419	Wickham	DMBS	109	E	2-car units
50420-423	Birmingham	DMBS	104	M	3-car units
50424-427	Birmingham	DMC(L)	104	M	3-car units
50428-479	Birmingham	DMBS	104	M	3-car units
50480-531	Birmingham	DMC(L)	104	M	3-car units

No series	Built	Type	Class	Regions Allocated	Notes
50532-541	Birmingham	DMBS	104	M	2-car units
50542-593	Birmingham	DMC(L)	104	E	4-car units
50594-598	Birmingham	DMBS	104	E	2-car units
50599-629	Derby	DMBS	108	E	2 or 3-car units
50630-646	Derby	DMC(L)	108	E	3 or 4-car units
50647-695	Swindon	DMS(L)	120	W	Cross-Country 3-car units
50696-744	Swindon	DMBC	120	W	Cross-Country 3-car units
50745-751	Met-Cam	DMC(L)	101	E	3 or 4-car units
50752-784	Cravens	DMBS	105	M	2 or 3-car units
50785-817	Cravens	DMC(L)	105	M	2 or 3-car units
50818-870	Derby	DMBS	116	M/W	Suburban 3-car
50871-923	Derby	DMS	116	M/W	Suburban 3-car
50924-935	Derby	DMBS	108	M	2-car units
50936	Swindon	DMS(L)	126	Sc	Inter City 6-car units
50938-987	Derby	DMBS	108	M	2-car units
50988-1007	Derby	DMS	125	E	Suburban 3-car
51008-029	Swindon	DMS(L)	126	Sc	Inter City 6-car units
51030-051	Swindon	DMBS	126	Sc	Inter City 3 or 6-car units
51052-079	Gloucester	DMBC	119	M/W	Cross-Country 3-car units
51080-107	Gloucester	DMS(L)	119	M/W	Cross-Country 3-car units
51108-127	Gloucester	DMBS	100	Sc	2-car units
51128-140	Derby	DMBS	116	M/W	Suburban 3-car
51141-153	Derby	DMS	116	M/W	Suburban 3-car
51154-173	Derby	DMBS	125	E	Suburban 3-car
51174-253	Met-Cam	DMBS	101	M/E/Sc	2-car units
51254-301	Cravens	DMBS	105	E	2-car units
51302-316	Birmingham	DMBS	118	W	Suburban 3-car
51317-331	Birmingham	DMS	118	W	Suburban 3-car
51332-373	Pressed St	DMBS	117	W	Suburban 3-car
51374-415	Pressed St	DMS	117	W	Suburban 3-car

Right: **A pair of Class 116 units forms the 3pm Merthyr to Cardiff General service leaves Taffs Well station under the watchful eye of the signalman in his lofty box on 17 February 1962.** *Andrew F. Smith*

No series	Built	Type	Class	Regions Allocated	Notes
51416-424	Derby	DMBS	108	M	2-car units
51425-470	Met-Cam	DMBS	101	E/Sc	3 or 4 car units
51471-494	Cravens	DMBS	105	E/Sc	2-car units
51495-540	Met-Cam	DMC(L)	101	E/Sc	2, 3 or 4 car units
51541-550	Met-Cam	DMBS	111	E	2 or 3-car units
51551-560	Met-Cam	DMC(L)	111	E	2 or 3-car units
51561-572	Derby	DMC(L)	108	M	4-car Suburban
51573-581	Swindon	DMBC(L)	120	W	Cross-Country 3-car units
51582-590	Swindon	DMS(L)	120	W	Cross-Country 3-car units
51591-650	Derby	DMBS	127	M	Suburban 4-car
51651-680	Derby	DMBS	115	M	Suburban 4-car
51681-705	Cravens	DMBS	112	M	2-car units
51706-730	Cravens	DMC(L)	112	M	2-car units
51731-755	Cravens	DMBS	113	M	2-car units
51756-780	Cravens	DMC(L)	113	M	2-car units
51781/2/7	Swindon	DMBC	120	Sc	Cross-Country 3-car
51783-786	Swindon	DMBF	120	Sc	Cross-Country 3-car
51788-794	Swindon	DMS(L)	120	Sc	Cross-Country 3-car
51795-801	Met-Cam	DMBS	101	Sc	3-car units
51802-808	Met-Cam	DMC(L)	101	Sc	3-car units
51809-828	Birmingham	DMBC	110	E	3-car units
51829-848	Birmingham	DMC(L)	110	E	3-car units
51849-900	Derby	DMBS	115	M	Suburban 4-car
51901-950	Derby	DMBS	108	M	2-car units
51951-967	Swindon	DMC	124	E	Trans Pennine 6-car units
51968-984	Swindon	MBS(K)	124	E	Trans Pennine 6-car units
51985-2010	Derby	DMBS	107	Sc	3-car units
52011-036	Derby	DMC(L)	107	Sc	3-car units
52037-065	Derby	DMC(L)	108	M	2-car units
52066-075	Birmingham	DMBS	110	M	3-car units
52076-085	Birmingham	DMC(L)	110	M	3-car units
52086-095	Swindon	DMBS(L)	123	W	Inter City 4-car
52096-105	Swindon	DMS(K)	123	W	Inter City 4-car
55000-019	Gloucester	DMBS	122	M/W	Single units
55020-035	Pressed St	DMBS	121	W	Single units
55987-996	Gloucester	DMPV	128	M	Parcels vans
55997-999	Cravens	DMPV	129	M	Parcels vans
56000-049	Derby	DTC(L)	114	E	2-car units
56050-089	Met-Cam	DTC(L)	101	E/M	2-car units
56090-093	Met-Cam	DTC(L)	111	E/M	2-car units
56094-113	Gloucester	DTC(L)	100	M/Sc	2-car units
56114-149	Cravens	DTC(L)	105	E	2-car units
56150-169	Park Royal	DTC(L)	103	M	2-car units
56170-174	Wickham	DTC(L)	109	E	2-car units
56175-189	Birmingham	DTC(L)	104	M/E	2-car units
56190-215	Derby	DTC(L)	108	E/M/	2-car units
56218-220	Met-Cam	DTC(L)	101	NE	2-car units
56221-279	Derby	DTC(L)	108	M	2-car units
56280-289	Pressed St	DTS	121	W	2-car units
56291-299	Gloucester	DTS	122	M/W	Single unit trailers
56300-319	Gloucester	DTC(L)	100	Sc	2-car units
56332-411	Met-Cam	DTC(L)	101	M/E/Sc	2-car units
56412-483	Cravens	DTC(L)	105	E/Sc	2-car units
56484-504	Derby	DTC(L)	108	M	2-car units
59000-031	Derby	TC	116	M	Suburban 3-car
59032-041	Derby	TS	116	W	Suburban 3-car
59042-048	Met-Cam	TS(L)	101	E	4-car units
59049-055	Met-Cam	TBS(L)	101	E	4-car units
59060-072	Met-Cam	TS(L)	101	E	4-car units
59073-085	Met-Cam	TBS(L)	101	E	4-car units
59086-091	Met-Cam	TS(L)	101	E	4-car units
59092-097	Met-Cam	TBS(L)	101	E	4-car units
59098-099	Swindon	TBuF(K)(L)	126	Sc	Inter City 3 or 6-car
59100-109	Met-Cam	TS(L)	101	E	3-car units
59112-113	Met-Cam	TBS(L)	101	E	4-car units

No series	Built	Type	Class	Regions Allocated	Notes
59114-131	Met-Cam	TC(L)	101	M	3-car units
59132-187	Birmingham	TC(L)	104	M	3-car units
59188-208	Birmingham	TS(L)	104	E	4-car units
59209-229	Birmingham	TBS(L)	104	E	4-car units
59230-234	Birmingham	TS(L)	104	E	4-car units
59235-239	Swindon	TS(L)	123	W	Inter City 4-car
59240-244	Birmingham	TBS(L)	104	E	4-car units
59245-250	Derby	TBS(L)	108	E	4-car units
59255-301	Swindon	TBuS(L)	120	W	Cross-Country 3-car
59302-306	Met-Cam	TS(L)	101	E	3 or 4-car units
59307-325	Cravens	TS(L)/TC(L)	105		M 3-car units
59326-376	Derby	TC	116	M/W	Suburban 3-car
59380-390	Derby	TS(L)	108	E	3 or 4-car units
59391-400	Swindon	TF(K)	126	Sc	Inter-City units
59402-412	Swindon	TC(L)	126	Sc	Inter-City units
59413-437	Gloucester	TBuS(L)	119	M/W	Cross-Country 3-car
59438-448	Derby	TC	116	M/W	Suburban 3-car
59449-468	Derby	TS	125	E	Suburban 3-car
59469-483	Birmingham	TC(L)	118	W	Suburban 3-car
59484-522	Pressed St	TC(L)	117	W	Suburban 3-car
59523-568	Met-Cam	TC(L)	101	E/Sc/W	3 or 4-car units
59569-572	Met-Cam	TS(L)	101	E	3-car units
59573-578	Met-Cam	TBuS(L)	111	E	4-car units
59579-588	Swindon	TBuS(L)	120	W	Cross-Country 3-car
59589-618	Derby	TS(L)	127	M	Suburban 4-car
59619-648	Derby	TS	127	M	Suburban 4-car
59649-663	Derby	TS	115	M	Suburban 4-car
59664-678	Derby	TC(L)	115	M	Suburban 4-car
59679-685	Swindon	TBuS(L)	120	Sc	Cross-Country 3-car
59686-692	Met-Cam	TC(L)	101	Sc	3-car units
59693-712	Birmingham	TS(L)	110	E	3-car units
59713-718	Derby	TS	115	M	Suburban 4-car
59719-724	Derby	TC(L)	115	M	Suburban 4-car
59725-744	Derby	TS	115	M	Suburban 4-car
59745-764	Derby	TC(L)	115	M	Suburban 4-car
59765-773	Swindon	TS(L)	124	E	Trans-Pennine 6-car units
59774-781	Swindon	TBuF(L)	124	E	Trans-Pennine 6-car units
59782-807	Derby	TS(L)	107	Sc	3-car units
59808-817	Birmingham	TS(L)	110	M	3-car units
59818-827	Swindon	TC(K)	123	W	Inter City 4-car units
59828-832	Swindon	TSRB(L)	123	W	Inter City 4-car units
79000-007	Derby	DMBS	—		Withdrawn 2-car units
79008-046	Derby	DMBS	—	E/M	2-car units
79047-082	Met-Cam	DMBS	—	E	2-car units
79083-111	Swindon	DMBS(L)	—	Sc	Inter City 3 or 6-car units
79118-149	Derby	DMBS	—	E/M	2-car units
79150-154	Derby	DMS	—		Withdrawn 4-car units
79155-168	Swindon	DMS(L)	—	Sc	Inter City 6-car units
79169-181	Derby	DMBS	—	M	2-car units
79184-188	Derby	DMBS	—	M	2-car units
79189-190	Derby	DMC(L)	—	M	2-car units
79191-193	Derby	DTC(L)	—	M	Renumbered 79633-635
79250-262	Derby	DTC(L)	—	E/M	2-car units
79263-291	Met-Cam	DTS(L)	—	E	2-car units
79325-329	Derby	TBS(L)	—		Withdrawn 4-car units
79400-404	Derby	TS(L)	—		Withdrawn 4-car units
79440-447	Swindon	TBuF(K)	—	Sc	Inter-City 3 or 6-car units
79470-482	Swindon	TF(K)	—	Sc	Inter-City 3 or 6-car units
79500-507	Derby	DMC(L)	—		Withdrawn 2-car units
79508-512	Derby	DMC	—		Withdrawn 4-car units
79600-625	Derby	DTC(L)	—	M	2-car units
79626-632	Met-Cam	DTC(L)	—	E/M	2-car units
79633-635	Derby	DTC(L)	—	M	2-car units
79639-684	Derby	DTC(L)	—	M	2-car units

No series	Built	Type	Class	Regions Allocated	Notes
79740	ACV (BUT)	DMS	—		Withdrawn 3-car/4-wheel unit
79741	ACV (BUT)	TS	—		Withdrawn 3-car/4-wheel unit
79742-744	ACV (BUT)	DMBS	—		Withdrawn 3-car/4-wheel unit
79745	ACV (BUT)	DMS	—		Withdrawn 3-car/4-wheel unit
79746-747	ACV (BUT)	TS	—		Withdrawn 3-car/4-wheel unit
79748	ACV (BUT)	DMS	—		Withdrawn 3-car/4-wheel unit
79749	ACV (BUT)	TS	—		Withdrawn 3-car/4-wheel unit
79750	ACV (BUT)	DMBS	—		Withdrawn 3-car/4-wheel unit
79900-901	Derby	DMBS	—		Withdrawn Single units
79958-959	Bristol	Railbus	—		Withdrawn 4-wheel Railbus
79960-964	W&M	Railbus	—		Withdrawn 4-wheel Railbus
79965-969	Wickham	Railbus	—		Withdrawn 4-wheel Railbus
79970-974	Park Royal	Railbus	—	Sc	4-wheel Railbus
79975-979	AC Cars	Railbus	—	Sc	4-wheel Railbus

Diesel-Electric Multiple-Units

No series	Built	Type	Class	Regions Allocated	Notes
60000-013	Eastleigh	DMBS	201	S	Hastings units
60014-031	Eastleigh	DMBS	202	S	Hastings units
60032-045	Eastleigh	DMBS	203	S	Hastings units
60100-125	Eastleigh	DMBS	205	S	Hampshire units
60126-144	Eastleigh	DMBS	207	S	East Sussex units
60145-151	Eastleigh	DMBS	205	S	Hampshire units
60500-520	Eastleigh	TS(L)	201	S	Hastings units
60521-547	Eastleigh	TS(L)	202	S	Hastings units
60548-561	Eastleigh	TS(L)	203	S	Hastings units
60600-618	Eastleigh	TC(L)	207	S	East Sussex units
60650-678	Eastleigh	TS	205	S	Hampshire units
60700-706	Eastleigh	TFK(L)	201	S	Hastings units
60707-715	Eastleigh	TFK(L)	202	S	Hastings units
60716-722	Eastleigh	TFK(L)	203	S	Hastings units
60750-756	Eastleigh	TRBu	203	S	Hastings units
60800-832	Eastleigh	DTC(L)	205	S	Hampshire units
60900-918	Eastleigh	DTS	207	S	East Sussex units
60090-093	Met-Cam	DMBF(L)	—	W	Pullman 6-car units
60094-099	Met-Cam	DMBS	—	W	Pullman 8-car units
60644-649	Met-Cam	DMBS(L)	—	W	Pullman 8-car units
60730-733	Met-Cam	TKF(L)	—	W	Pullman 6-car units
60734-739	Met-Cam	TKF(L)	—	W	Pullman 8-car units
60740-749	Met-Cam	TPF(L)	—	W	Pullman 6 or 8-car units

Battery-Electric Railcars (included as based on DMU bodywork)

No series	Built	Type	Class	Regions Allocated	Notes
79998	Derby/Cowlairs	DMBS	—		Withdrawn 2-car units
79999	Derby/Cowlairs	DTC	—		Withdrawn 2-car units

KEY TO TYPE

TBu	Trailer Buffet
TFK	Trailer First (Side) Corridor
TBuS	Trailer Buffet Second
TSLRB	Trailer Second Restaurant Buffet with lavatory
TBS	Trailer Brake Second
TS	Trailer Second
DTC	Driving Trailer Composite (First and Second class accommodation)
DTS	Driving Trailer Second
TC	Trailer Composite (First and Second class accommodation)
DMPV	Driving Motor Parcels Van
DMBS	Driving Motor Brake Second
DMS	Driving Motor Second
DMC	Driving Motor Composite
L	Lavatory compartment within vehicle
TPF	Trailer Parlour First (Pullman)
TKF	Trailer Kitchen First (Pullman)
MKF	Motor Kitchen First (Pullman)
DMBS	Driving Motor Brake Second (Pullman)
DMBF	Driving Motor Brake First (Pullman)

Note: When first introduced Third class was in use, redesignated Second in 1956 and now referred to as Standard

COUPLING CODES

Variations in types of transmission meant that not all units could work together. To distinguish units that could run together, the different control systems were coded as follows to ensure that only compatible vehicles were coupled tegether:

Red Triangle —Derby 'Lightweights' fitted with 125hp engine and torque converter; also Derby /Rolls-Royce four-car suburban Class 127

Yellow Diamond — Derby 'Lightweight' and Metropolitan-Cammell units fitted with 150hp engine and Wilson gearbox, and Cravens Class 129 parcels cars.

White Circle — Swindon Inter-City units for Scottish Region and Swindon Inter-City Class 126 units.

Orange Star — Derby three-car suburban Class 125 units.

Blue Square — All other standard transmission stock with AEC, Leyland or Rolls-Royce engines.

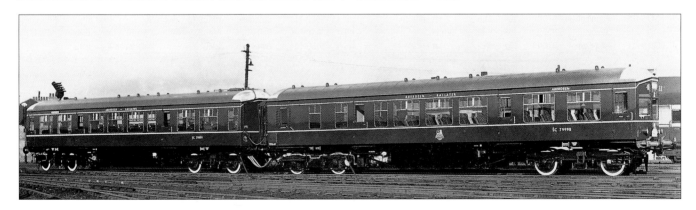

Above: **Nos Sc79998 and Sc79999 were a pair of battery powered railcars, the bodywork of which is clearly based on the contemporary Derby 'Lightweight' design. The give away was the lack of an obvious engine between the bogies. Two electric motors were provided in one of the motor coaches and the set was used on the Aberdeen–Ballater service. Little appears to have been published on the workings but they may be considered not to have been completely successful as the type was not duplicated. The weight of the batteries would no doubt have been a considerable disadvantage. They were withdrawn in December 1966 and entered Departmental stock as Nos DB975003 and 975004, being used by the Railway Technical Centre (RTC) at Derby. This included use on cab signalling trials during the 1970s on the Old Dalby test track. Happily, they are now preserved on the Royal Deeside Railway.** *BR*

SOUTHERN REGION DEMUS

Left: The tradition in books on diesel units has, in the past, appeared to dictate that the Eastleigh-built DEMUs are covered towards the end of the work. Having had the 'misfortune' to be subjected to countless hours and miles as a passenger in these things, I am happy to deal with them at the beginning this time. The first such vehicles to appear were the six-coach 'Hastings' units, introduced in 1957, built to the restricted width dictated by the loading gauge for that line. The success of these units allowed the complete dieselisation of services over the route; so much so that eventually 23 six-coach sets were delivered and which remained basically intact until 1964, when three sets were disbanded with their coaches used to form part of the 'Tadpole' series.

An original formation of two six-coach Hastings sets is seen at Hither Green, unit No 1002 trailing, with a total of 2,400hp available for what was a 12-coach train. It was near this location in 1967 that a broken rail caused a major derailment of a Hastings line service with considerable loss of life. *P. J. Sharpe*

Left: Unit No 1015 enters Crowhurst on a semi-fast working in the late 1950s. Much of the infrastructure in the picture had changed little from the steam era; the semaphore signalling and wonderful pole-route were yet to succumb to modernisation. *P. J. Sharpe*

Left: A publicity view of the interior of a second class saloon from a Hastings unit in 1957. The fashions of the period are themselves worthy of a second glance. Cleverly positioned nearest the camera, the two women of slight build give the appearance of plenty of space. In practice the seating was often a squash for those of more generous proportions. Notice, too, the passenger smoking, this being the period before such a habit was considered socially unacceptable in what was an advertisement for the railway. *BR*

Right: The cab layouts of the various DEMUs were basically similar, regardless of type. The cab of this Hastings DEMU features a master controller, as seen in the driver's right hand, graduated to various notches and which also had to be kept depressed as the 'dead-man's handle'. The spring on the controller could be quite stiff and it was not unknown for a driver to relax his grip for an instant, in which case the controller had to be fully closed before it could be opened again. The wonderfully responsive Southern Region (SR) type of 'EP' (electro-pneumatic) brake was also fitted. *BR*

Below: Meanwhile, later in 1957, Eastleigh had also been busy building the first batch of 18 two-car diesel-electric units for branch line use. These 'Hampshire' units were also a total success so that the series was eventually extended further to a total of 33 sets, with most later also being given a third coach. Unit No 1114 is depicted in what was then Platform 2 at Eastleigh.

In later years, one counterpoint to the commercial success of these units, however, was the constant low frequency noise generated which resulted in some crews claiming against BR for damage to their hearing. *P. J. Sharpe*

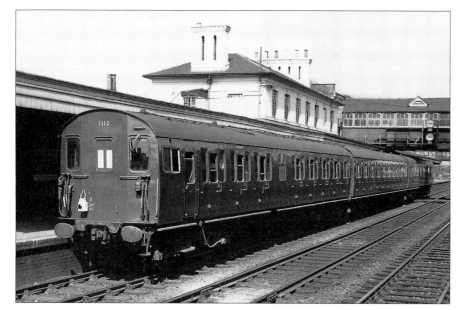

Above: **This is the same location as the previous picture, but this time with unit No 1110 strengthened to a three-car set, which took place in 1959. When originally built the power car was rated at just 500hp which meant that even on full throttle it was rarely possible to achieve much more than 50mph on the gently rising gradient north of Eastleigh. The heavier gradients of the Mid-Hants line also caused problems for these sets and, accordingly, it was the practice for two-car units to be used on most services on this line.**
P. J. Sharpe

Below: **The 'Hampshire' units gradually took over the majority of branch and cross-country workings on the former Southern lines in Hampshire and Berkshire and so allowed for the withdrawal of a number of steam classes, notably the 'M7' class 0-4-4Ts and various Drummond 4-4-0 types. Main line workings through Hampshire, however, remained almost entirely steam hauled and so for many years it was a common sight to witness a DEMU alongside a Bulleid Pacific. Such was the scene at Southampton Central on 7 August 1965, unit No 1131 having been given the road east towards St Denys and its eventual destination at Portsmouth with the 12.21 departure, while 'West Country' No 34047 *Callington* heads the 12.15 to Waterloo and waits impatiently.** *A. D. McIntyre*

Left: Red moquette was originally used in second class and a dark blue for the first class compartments. Seating was in a three-plus-two arrangement which could become a bit cramped. There was just one toilet available to second class passengers per set and this was only accessible if travelling in the driving trailer as there were no corridor connections fitted between coaches. The 1960s witnessed two separate homicides in these sets, both occurring within the toilet area of the vehicle concerned. *BR*

Upper right: Access to the power unit, which was placed above rather than below the floor, was either alongside, via a narrow corridor, or if more major work was required, through a removable roof panel. The power unit was built by English Electric and had a cast-iron framework. This contributed to the 56-ton weight of the motor coach compared with the 32 tons of the driving trailer. In later years the engine blocks in some vehicles were found to have become porous in places, which eventually led to the withdrawal of a number of the class. *IAL*

Right: On 12 October 1964, unit No 1113 passes Southcote Junction signalbox near Reading with the 15.53 Reading General to Southampton Terminus service. Eleven stops later it will arrive at its destination. *J. Spencer Gilks*

Left:
Unit No 1121 was almost permanently allocated to the Eastern section of the SR and retained its original two-coach formation. It is seen here forming the 2.40pm Ashford to Hastings service at Appledore on 21 February 1961.
M. Edwards

Left: **Although SR DEMUs were able to work in multiple, albeit only with other SR DEMU types, it was nevertheless unusual to see many instances of such workings. On one such occasion at St Denys set No 1104 and a three-car set together form the 12.38pm Portsmouth & Southsea to Southampton as they leave the station on the last leg of their journey on 31 October 1959.** *J. C. Haydon*

Right: **Although spending the majority of their lives in the area for which they were intended, it was not unknown for a '13xx' set to be put on an Eastleigh working, this usually occurring following overhaul or repair. No 1310 is seen in the summer of 1962 at Platform 5 at Salisbury on a return Southampton–Portsmouth train.** *P. J. Sharpe*

Right: **Following on from the success of the 'Hampshire' units, 19 'East Sussex' or 'Oxted' line units were built in 1962. One variation was the lavatory compartment which was placed centrally within the middle carriage of the 'East Sussex' units, but again, as there were no gangways between vehicles, access was limited. Having three coaches and a 600hp engine from new, they were an improvement on the previous designs from the outset. However, due to different engine mountings the power units were not interchangeable with the earlier designs. Brand-new at Eastleigh on 10 March 1962, No 1301, the first of the new sets, reposes in the spring sunshine.** *Les Elsey*

Left: **As the name implies, the DEMU sets were intended for use on specific routes, the body design of the 'East Sussex' units being a compromise between the narrow Hastings line units and the standard loading gauge of the 'Hampshire' units. Adorned in the then-standard all-over green livery, which suited the sets so well, No 1309 stands at Tunbridge Wells West forming the 9.45am Eastbourne to Tonbridge working on 7 July 1962.** *D. S. Pollard*

Right: **Working on the Oxted line services meant that, apart from the six-coach 'Hastings' sets, the '13xx' series vehicles were the first three-coach DEMUs to be seen regularly at a London terminus. No 1313 is outside Victoria when almost new, at a time when regulations still required the use of an old-fashioned oil tail-lamp.** *P. J. Sharpe*

Left: **With Maunsell and Bulleid EMUs on either side, No 1309 runs through Clapham Junction sometime in the early 1960s. The work of the BR design panel was evident in these units, particularly with their recessed jumpers and more curved roof line. Even so, the flat front presented a rather bland and functional slab appearance.** *P. J. Sharpe*

Left: **Changing traffic patterns meant the original number of Hastings six-car units was already more than was sufficient for the Kent line by the mid-1960s. Accordingly, three of the original short-framed Class 201 sets were withdrawn as six-car sets and instead reformed into six three-car units comprising a motor coach, non-driving trailer and with a spare driving trailer from a former electric 2EPB set added. The result was a visually strange unit with two narrow-bodied vehicles and a wider coach — hence the nickname 'Tadpole'. Despite what was clearly a compromise solution the sets performed well and saw much service on the former Reading–Redhill–Tonbridge route. Unit No 1204 is seen leaving Redhill with the 13.04 to Tonbridge on 12 March 1965.** *J. Scrace*

Right:
The opposite, 'head' end of unit No 1204. Southern Region compatibility had meant that little modification was required to what had formerly been the driving trailer of an EMU, both diesel and electric designs using the excellent EP braking system. Originally outshopped in the then standard green livery, they later carried plain blue and finally corporate blue/grey. *IAL*

RAILBUSES

Right: **Arguably the first modern diesel unit to operate on BR after nationalisation was the privately sponsored ACV Demonstration train of 1952. It had bodywork by Park Royal and an AEC engine (as fitted to contemporary road buses), and was assembled by BUT. This bold attempt on a radical theme, despite its ultra-modern appearance for the period, was hardly attractive and understandably gained the nickname 'flying brick'. The ride, too, was best described as truly awful, although this did not prevent the LMR eventually operating three such sets from 1955 onwards. Originally painted in grey and red, the livery was later changed to standard DMU green, in which form all were eventually withdrawn in 1959. They then lingered at Derby until cut up four years later.** *IAL*

Right: **Nos M79900 and M79190 are seen at Potton in 1966. No M79190 was a standard Derby 'Lightweight' vehicle, a DMBTL from a two/four-coach set, but compatibility of coupling types — both yellow diamond — enabled it to operate with M79900, one of the Derby single-car units, although of course through access was not possible for passengers between the vehicles.** *P. R. Foster*

Right: **Seen at Witham (Essex) on 5 October 1963 is No E79963, a Waggon & Maschinenbau single-unit vehicle, one of five such supplied to BR in April 1958. Intended as a saviour to reduce operating costs on lightly used lines, the introduction of these vehicles did little to assist in the retention of services on various East Anglian branches — excepting that from Witham to Braintree — and accordingly four of the type later migrated to former NER and LMR lines, although again with singular lack of success. Fortunately only one of the vehicles was scrapped and the remaining four were acquired by preservationists, and have now been working for their new owners considerably longer than for BR.**
A. Swain/Transport Treasury

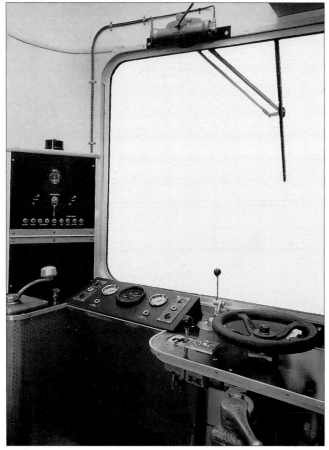

Above: **BR purchased a number of four-wheel railbuses including five built by Wickham, a manufacturer better known for its numerous motorised permanent way trolleys. No Sc79965, destined for the Scottish Region, is posed shortly after completion in 1958 outside Wickham's works at Ware in Hertfordshire.** *D. Wickham & Co Ltd*

Centre right: **Five small vehicles weighing just 11 tons each were also built by AC Cars Ltd and supplied to BR in February 1958. Having just 46 seats, it was hoped that much in the way of savings could be achieved with the use of these railbuses. However not enough reduction could be made in permanent way maintenance and operating costs altered little whilst revenue rarely increased much. This would certainly appear to have been the case at Crieff on 20 March 1959, where No Sc79979 forms what appears to be a lightly patronised 12.00 service to Gleneagles.** *E. J. Dew*

Left: **The basic cab layout of the Wickham railbus which had a semi-automatic gearbox selector, similar to that fitted to contemporary road buses.** *D. Wickham & Co Ltd*

Right: **A well-patronised Park Royal-built railbus, No Sc79970, is seen at Craigellachie, the junction of the lines from Keith, Boat of Garten and Elgin. Today, Craigellachie is devoid of a railway connection although the Keith & Dufftown Railway Association does reach as far as nearby Dufftown.** *P. J. Sharpe*

Right: **On the Western Region the AC-design vehicles were first used on the two stub end branches from Kemble to Tetbury and Cirencester although later they could be seen on shuttle workings from Bodmin and Yeovil. All of the type were also fitted with steps which could be swung out to allow access from low-height platforms, a commendable attempt at increasing patronage from a lineside stopping place where the construction of a full height platform was not warranted. This was of course a direct copy of earlier GWR practice with the provision of numerous wayside stopping places, when a number of auto-coaches had been similarly fitted with steps.** *P. H. Groom*

MODERNISATION PLAN DMUs

Left: **The first truly modern DMU units for British Railways were the '79xxx' series Derby 'Lightweight' units, consisting of just eight two-car sets. Although popular with the travelling public, the mechanics of the units were outdated even before they emerged, being based on the 1938 LMS/ Leyland engine and transmission. The vehicles in this first batch of Derby 'Lightweights' with 125hp engines were coupling code classified Red Triangle. As such, the sets would remain non-standard, leading to their early withdrawal in 1964.** *L. King*

Left: **The old and the new at Marylebone on 29 April 1954, with a pair of the Red Triangle Derby 'Lightweight' two-car sets on a demonstration run as far as Beaconsfield. Officially the sets were not brought into service until November 1954 but assuming the date quoted on the reverse of the photograph is correct, then certainly at least two units were operating trials some time earlier.** *Fox Photos*

Above right: **The second batch of Derby 'Lightweights' built in 1954 had 150hp engines fitted and were given Yellow Diamond coupling code. A six-car diesel set from this batch with Derby twin Motor Brake Second No E79139 leading is seen at Thirsk on 21 May 1959. The service is an up stopping train bound for York.** *Brian Morrison*

Left: **No E79041, a Driving Motor Brake Trailer from the original Yellow Diamond 1954 Derby build, is seen on a Norwich service. Livery at this time was still overall green but with a grey roof and yellow whiskers. This combination was arguably the most attractive the sets ever carried although in service the roofs quickly weathered to black, aided by the vertical exhausts which would also stain the roof of neighbouring vehicles. It came as no surprise when black roofs became standard shortly afterwards.** *P. J. Sharpe*

Below: **Units built by Metro-Cammell with a 150hp engine were also given the Yellow Diamond coupling code. A two-car Metro-Cammell unit works an Ipswich service, when quite new.** *IAL*

Above: **To gauge the structural integrity of the body shell design of the Metro-Cammell Bury–Bacup stock, weights were added to test for stress and distortion. The amount of weight involved here is not recorded although it is certainly considerable. Although the majority of the original 36 Metro-Cammell lightweights had been allocated to East Anglia, seven went to the LMR Bury–Bacup route.** *BR*

Above: **The interior of the first class compartment of a Metro-Cammell unit is seen, again Bury–Bacup stock, with the colour originally recorded as blue with blue carpets. This official photograph is dated 14 March 1956.** *BR*

Left: **The driver's compartment of a Metro-Cammell unit (Bury–Bacup stock, February 1956) with the handbrake and master switch visible. Blinds were provided in most of the units for night-time, although their use would often frustrate the enthusiastic late-night traveller hopeful of a good view ahead.** *BR*

Below: **First of the Cravens single-unit parcels cars, Class 129, three of which were built in July 1958. Having a total engine capacity of 300hp, the single vehicles were easily capable of hauling a limited trailing load but could also be seen attached to other Yellow Diamond coded vehicles when the need arose. Lining on the vehicles was cream whilst the circular coaching stock crest was carried. A commodious guards compartment, which could be used for further parcels, was provided at one end.** *IAL*

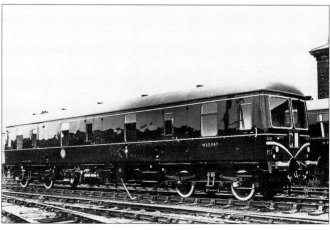

Right: **In 1956, BR Swindon Works produced 21 three-coach sets for Inter City use. The design was unusual in that at one end of the set there was a 'leading' car with a full-width driver's cab, as shown, while at the opposite end of the set there was an 'intermediate' driving motor car with a small cab on the left-hand side and an end corridor connection. This enabled two sets to be formed into a six-coach train with full through access for passengers. The units were given their own coupling code, White Circle. Modern-style open seating was provided for second class, although the traditional side corridor was retained for first class compartments. A number of the sets incorporated a buffet facility. Photographed when probably brand-new, this DMBS car displays the stencil which refers to it working a Class 'A' service.** *BR*

Below: **Viewed from the side, Swindon unit DMBSL No Sc79098 shows the curtains fitted to what was the second class accommodation. This car has been fitted with an additional windscreen wiper. These units were intended for use on both the Scottish and Western regions but all were later transferred for use north of the border. Their riding qualities were often subject to criticism although they were likely to be an improvement on those previously experienced in a locomotive-hauled train perhaps 20-30 years of age.** *BR*

Left: **The interior of the buffet area on one of the Swindon sets allocated to the Scottish Region in 1957, for use on the Glasgow–Edinburgh service. A variety of refreshments is available including beverages in proper cups. The infamous British Railways sandwiches will also be noted!** *BR*

Right: **In the area to which the units eventually migrated, a Swindon set with DMBSL No Sc79103 leading passes Cadder Yard on 18 August 1962. In the background 'V2' class 2-6-2 No 60929 waits to leave with a freight.** *S. Rickard*

Below: **A brand-new six-coach Swindon 'Inter-City' set on test on 31 July 1956 prior to being sent north. It is seen at High Wycombe passing the 4.10pm Paddington to Birmingham and Birkenhead service train, near Middle signalbox.** *R. M. Newland*

Left: **As originally built, the units had no means of train identification when the corridor end was leading. This was later modified to allow first for a single letter either side of the corridor blank and, later still, a pair of digits on each side thus complying with the four-digit headcode. The train is the 8.10am Birmingham Snow Hill to Carmarthen which is seen passing Acocks Green on 16 June 1959.** *M. Mensing*

Right: **The Swindon-built 'Inter-City' units saw extensive service on the Scottish Region and were initially intended for use between Edinburgh and Glasgow, a total of 21 three-coach sets being allocated to the region. One of these Glasgow–Edinburgh services is seen here, with a six-coach formation in 1958. Unfortunately, the lack of set numbers carried by DMUs at this time often makes identification impossible as the coach side numbers are not always visible.** *P. J. Sharpe*

STANDARD BLUE SQUARE COUPLING CODE DMUS

The next series of DMUs to be looked at comprises a number of similar — although by no means identical — units, most of which shared the same coupling code — Blue Square. Built from 1956 onwards, numerically, these units would make up the largest number of similar-styled trains running on BR, and at their peak were to be found almost throughout the length and breadth of the former BR system. Vehicles were constructed at the British Railways Works at Derby and Swindon, as well as by private manufacturers Birmingham Railway Carriage & Wagon Company (BRCW), Cravens, Gloucester Railway Carriage & Wagon Company (GRCW), Metropolitan-Cammell, Park Royal Vehicles, Pressed Steel and D. Wickham & Co.

Upper left: **Glasgow Central plays host to a Derby-built TOPS Class 107 unit. These Derby 'Heavyweights' were introduced to Scottish local services in 1960/1.** *P. J. Sharpe*

Left: **A Derby three-car Class 107 set, including centre car TSL No Sc59782, on excursion duties from Glasgow near Fort William on 22 May 1961. A portion had been detached at Crianlarich for Oban. The line to the left leads to the British Aluminium Company works.** *M. Mensing*

Left: **Derby DMBS No M50986 forms part of a two-coach, 'Lightweight' unit, TOPS Class 108. Mechanical transmission was used for these sets which had two 150hp engines per vehicle. The set is seen at Northampton (Castle) waiting to leave for Bedford Midland Road on 17 June 1961 with the 6.7pm departure.** *M. Mensing*

Right: **Derby two-car 'Lightweights' were used for both suburban and branch line duties. Here a Class 108 set, with an SR PMV in tow, is seen having left Sandy on the Cambridge to Bletchley 4.47pm service on 7 August 1961.** *M. Mensing*

Below: **Westbound from Bath, a Western Region Derby three-car set has just left Twerton Tunnel and is destined for Weston-super-Mare on 18 May 1967.** *P. H. Groom*

Below: **The obvious benefit of coupling compatibility is shown here to advantage with a Derby 'Lightweight' coupled to a Birmingham RCW set approaching Prestbury on the 1.18pm Macclesfield Central to Manchester London Road working on Good Friday, 27 March 1959. An up train of Metro-Cammell stock passes from the left.** *M. Mensing*

Above: **A Derby 'Lightweight' two-car, later-design set, at Hunt's Cross on 19 September 1961 when working the 2.57pm Warrington Central to Liverpool Central service. DMBS No M50628 is leading.** *M. Mensing*

Below: **Unpowered Derby DTCL No M56265 leads this pairing en route from Llandudno to Llandudno Junction in August 1961.** *IAL*

Above: **TOPS Class 108 DMCL No 51562 was the 1,000th DMU car built at Derby Works and was marked by a brief ceremony in November 1959. It was the 414th 'Lightweight' car to be completed and the works manager, A. E. Bates, congratulated the staff on their achievement. This car is now preserved as part of the National Collection at York. It was seen at Wrexham Central on 2 July 1963 still carrying its commemorative carriage board.** *Leslie Sandler*

Right: **Maintaining the fleet: at what appears to be Allerton deopt, the pump is being used to collect old lubricating oil from the drum in the pit, which has been drained from the Derby 'Lightweight' unit.** *Megator Pumps & Compressors Ltd*

Above: **Derby DTCL No M56270, with the first class compartments to the front of the vehicle.** *P. J. Sharpe*

Upper right: **A Derby 'Heavyweight' Class 114 is recorded when almost new alongside the Ruston engine plant at Lincoln. Introduced from 1956 onwards, these were the first sets to be given numbers in the 5xxxx series, the 'Heavyweight' designation coming from the use of steel in place of aluminium for the bodies which resulted in a much more robust vehicle.** *IAL*

Below: **The driver's compartment of a Derby 'Heavyweight'. The main controller is operated by the driver's left hand; the gear selector and direction control is the similar handle to the right. To the right of this is the brake lever and the AWS acknowledgement plunger.** *IAL*

Centre right: **The power unit of a Derby two-car set for the Eastern Region — later Class 114 — which produced 460hp and a creditable power-to-weight ratio of 6.9hp per ton. This was necessary due to the relatively heavy weight of each set, which could be as much as 66 tons 10cwt empty.** *IAL*

Lower right: **The interior of Derby DTCL No E56037, showing the typical single-direction bus-type seats. It was photographed at Derby on 18 May 1976 between trips to Matlock, awaiting departure on the 12.17 service.** *P. J. Fowler*

Right: **Open Day at Marylebone — a DMBS from a Derby-built TOPS Class 115 unit awaits the visitors. The Hawksworth-design coach to the rear would not form part of the unit when in service!** *BR*

Below: **The unusual pairing of a Derby DMBS and DMPV, the combination forming the 4.45pm High Wycombe to Aylesbury service, is seen on 18 October 1962 near West Wycombe.** *H. K. Harman*

Right: **First class seating from a Marylebone-based Derby unit, although without antimacassars, as would be found in comparable contemporary locomotive-hauled compartment stock.** *BR*

Above: **Later classified as Class 116, the three-car Derby-built 'Heavyweight' sets were introduced from 1957 onwards, with some seeing almost 40 years of service. Depicted here for the official photographer on the Wirksworth branch — where a number of official views of the period were recorded — No W50092 leads TC No W59000 and DMBS No W50050 while undergoing trials before delivery to the Western Region.** *BR*

Left: **A three-car Derby suburban unit approaches Hatton Junction, which is showing a wonderful array of pointwork.** *P. J. Sharpe*

Right: **This Derby 'Heavyweight' three-coach set remains in almost as-built condition complete with marker lights. Eventually, the middle and upper lights were removed although the destination blind panel was retained. This change had taken place on all these sets by the late 1970s.** *P. J. Sharpe*

Upper right: **By the time this Derby trailer composite, No W59375 from a three-car set seen at Westbury on 27 March 1970, was photographed, it had been downgraded to second class only and repainted rail blue. Ten of the batch were constructed as TSs, the rest as TCs, all of which became second class only in the late '60s, both types weighing 28 tons 10cwt.** *D. L. Percival*

Centre right: **The three-coach Derby sets of the suburban type built for the Western Region first appeared in April 1957 with construction continuing through to 1958. This latter batch differed slightly in that a two-figure route indicator panel was fitted but these fell into disuse and were subsequently seen crudely plated over.** *P. J. Sharpe*

Below: **This Cardiff-based Derby suburban set seen on an Ebbw Vale service, clearly shows one of the underhung BUT (Leyland) power units, of which there were two per vehicle. At rest these engines were, to say the least, noisy although the gentle rocking of the coach was an excellent encouragement to sleep at the end of the day.** *P. J. Sharpe*

Left: **Derby DMBS No W50087 could seat 65 passengers in relative (dis)comfort as well as having separate accommodation for goods and also the guard.** *P. J. Sharpe*

Left: **Displaying the characteristic 'eyebrows' above the front windows, a three-car Derby suburban set approaches Pershore. It displays a small yellow warning panel on the ends.** *P. J. Sharpe*

Left: **An unusual pairing of a Derby suburban three-car set and a Gloucester diesel parcels car in the W5599X series. The combination was recorded at Lapworth on 20 September 1961, although one can only speculate as to why such a combination had resulted because the DMPVs usually worked alone.** *M. Mensing*

Right: **The guard appears to have opened his door perhaps a shade too early on this occasion, as the 10.3am Stratford-upon-Avon service from Birmingham Snow Hill arrives at Earlswood Lakes station on 31 May 1959.** *M. Mensing*

Above: **Heath Junction at Cardiff on 30 April 1958 sees the Derby suburban units already starting to replace pannier tanks on the local workings. This is the 4.24pm Rhymney to Cardiff Queen Street in the days before rationalisation had occurred**. *S. Rickard*

Right: **Still in basically originally condition, two WR Derby suburban units pass Cherry Orchard sidings, between Cefn On and Llanishen, on 19 August 1963.** *S. Rickard*

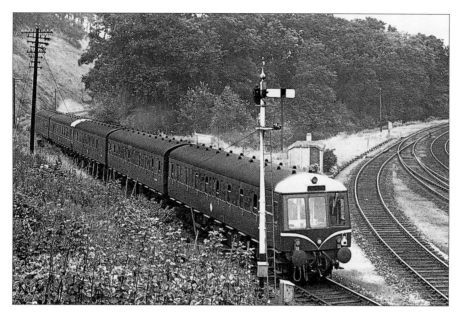

Left: **Part of the complex at Yeovil with its various junctions is portrayed here on 3 August 1963 as the 2pm (Sundays only) from Taunton leaves Yeovil Town for Yeovil Pen Mill.** *B. J. Ashworth*

Below: **Two WR Derby suburban units are seen here at Chippenham in September 1965, the second just visible standing on the running line in the distance. In the foreground, though, is the Calne branch service, depicted in its final days of operation, with DMBS No W51134 on the right.** *Paul Strong*

Left: **A rare sight in South Wales at the time: a pair of Derby two-car units forming a four-coach all-second service. This is the 11.42am (Saturdays only) Barry to Llantwit Major, passing Barry Sidings signalbox on the former Vale of Glamorgan route on 25 July 1959.** *S. Rickard*

Left: **The flexibility in working single units occasionally resulted in some unusual combinations, such as this approaching Rowington Junction near Lapworth on 12 April 1959. Two Gloucester single units are being led by a Derby Class 116 power car from a three-car set forming the 10am Wellington–Leamington Spa local.** *M. Mensing*

Below: **A Derby Class 125 three-car set leaves Lea Bridge and passes the northern end of an apparently empty Temple Mills Yard, with a 'Lea Valley' train bound for Stratford, on 14 June 1967. A Ruston & Hornsby industrial diesel shunter can be seen peeping over the wall of the works in the background.** *P. H. Groom*

Below: **In the blue era a Derby-built Class 125 unit with No E51162, by this time in blue livery, at the head leads a formation south through Potters Bar on the 09.12 Royston to King's Cross service, 6 December 1975. Class 125 Lea Valley units were given the unique Orange Star coupling code.** *Brian Morrison*

Above: **The Derby Class 127 four-coach suburban sets with hydraulic transmission were used on a number of London and Midlands high-density services including between St Pancras and Bedford. Each set accommodated no fewer than 328 seated passengers, 30 of which were first class. Two of the units are seen leaving Elstree & Borehamwood bound for the capital on 13 August 1960, forming the 3pm Bedford– St Pancras. Leading is DMBS No M51601.** *J. C. Haydon*

Left: **An LMR-based Derby-built hydraulic unit, forming the 2.35pm St Pancras to Kettering stopping service, approaches Elstree & Borehamwood, with DMBS No M51613 leading, on 14 September 1963. In service, this transmission was never as reliable as its mechanical counterpart, but these units remained in use for over 20 years although initially only intended as a 'stopgap' measure. Some even saw further service as dedicated parcels and newspaper vehicles.** *Brian Stephenson*

Left: **A combination of two four-car Derby Class 127 sets with Rolls-Royce engines, recorded on a St Pancras to Bedford working. When running correctly, each four-car set would produce 952hp output, although as referred to earlier, this was not always the case with the hydraulic transmission and often one power car would be taking more than its fair share of the load.** *BR*

Left: In pristine external condition, Derby Class 127 DMBS No M51635 stands at the end of a Rolls-Royce-powered, hydraulic four-car set at Bedford Midland Road, on 11 January 1960. *D. Kingston*

Left: A similar unit on trial on 28 August 1959 passes through St Albans City station at 2pm. Aside from such running-in turns, these workings were also used to introduce staff to the new trains, although on this occasion it would appear that only two men are present in the driving compartment. DMBS No M51594 is leading. *A. W. Besley*

Below: Posed for the official photographer, this side view of a Derby unit displays to advantage the compromise window/seating plan on these units. The necessity of affording ease of loading and unloading has resulted in pillars being provided in the space normally used by passengers for vision, with the seat ends set squarely in the middle of the largest windows. *BR*

Above: **Swindon-built TOPS Class 120 units were first introduced in 1957. Disturbing the peace on Sunday, 9 March 1958, the 9am six-car Swansea to Birmingham Snow Hill passes through the former GWR station at Evesham. This is the rear of the train which had been diverted via Ashchurch and Evesham due to engineering work on the line through Broadway.** *M. Mensing*

Left: **Two Swindon three-car sets coupled together form the 5.5pm from Birmingham Snow Hill to Swansea on 11 May 1961. They are seen approaching Acocks Green station with DMBC No W50716 leading and the second coach identifiable as a buffet vehicle.** *M. Mensing*

Right: **Another area within the West Midlands which was the haunt of the Swindon units was the line to Worcester from the Oxford direction. Here, a three-car set leaves Chipping Campden Tunnel with the 1.25pm Kingham to Worcester service on 15 June 1963.** *M. Mensing*

Left: **The old and the new: a Swindon 'Cross-country' set passes a pair of former GWR AEC single-unit diesel railcars north of Worcester on 27 August 1961. The three-car set is working the 2.40pm Birmingham Snow Hill to Cardiff service and has just turned on to the Foregate Street route.** *M. Mensing*

Right: **In the days prior to track, signalling and stock rationalisation, the 2.25pm Cardiff to Birmingham service approaches Pontypool Road station in March 1959. This view is typical of the era into which the first-generation DMUs entered. It shows a scene which had changed little over generations and yet was destined to be swept away within a few short years. The goods yard, lines of stock, bull-head track, mechanical signalling, rodding runs, ATC ramps and the like are now either totally abolished or reduced to odd pockets on secondary and lesser routes.** *S. Rickard*

Left: Another example of 'tail' traffic: the 4pm Birmingham Snow Hill to Hereford service near Stourbridge, between Cradley Heath and Lye, on 14 June 1958. Such working, meaning the addition of urgent traffic in the form of a fitted van or horsebox to the rear of a local train, had been commonplace during steam days. It was a method of operation which continued with the introduction of the diesel units, although by about 1962 it was rare. The reason for the decline was simply that station yards were closing and so such traffic was being lost. *M. Mensing*

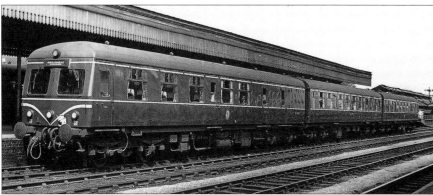

Left: Oxford station prior to rebuilding, with a three-coach Swindon set on what was probably a Birkenhead to Paddington working. The speedometer drive is displayed to advantage on the front wheel. *P. J. Sharpe*

Left: Another diverted Cardiff working is seen, this time at Ashchurch with an almost brand-new Swindon unit en route to Wales on 29 March 1958. The weight of each three-car set was in the order of 110 tons empty and with power provided from two 150hp engines per motor coach this gave a total of 600hp, a power-to-weight ratio in the order of 5.45hp per ton. This compared favourably with the former GWR units where the ratio was less than 4hp per ton when running with an additional centre coach. *R. Russell*

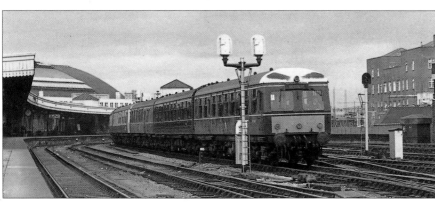

Left: The 12.50pm Bristol Temple Meads to Weston-super-Mare service is at the start of its journey on 31 October 1968. By this time most Class 120s had been repainted blue, or blue-and-grey as with the set behind, but the leading set was a late survivor in green. *P. J. Fowler*

Right: **Rescued by a pannier tank, a three-coach hybrid set of two Swindon power cars and a suburban trailer needs assistance in the Worcester area late in 1963. Failures of the sets were understandably more common in the early days, until both maintenance and operating staff became familiar with them. Even so, there were some odd, poorly designed features, one of which was the fact that each power car was a self-contained unit generating its own air supply which turn fed the air-horns for the vehicle. Thus, if the leading power car failed, the whole unit was considered non-operative as the leading end horns could not then be activated by air from the remaining working power unit.** *Anthony A. Vickers*

Below: **On the 'Withered Arm', the old Southern line west of Exeter, a three-coach Swindon set approaches Barnstaple Junction on a Torrington line working on 2 September 1965.** *P. H. Wells*

Left: **To complement the Swindon units on their longer cross-country workings, most had a centre buffet car, complete with the characteristic Formica panelling of the period. This is TSLRB No 59255.** *BR*

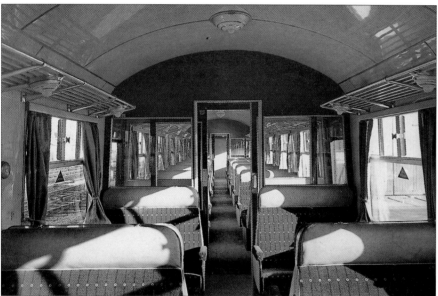

Left: **The remainder of the same trailer second buffet accommodated 60 second class seats. The weight of the vehicle empty was stated as 30 tons 12cwt.** *BR*

Below: **In addition to their normal workings, the Swindon sets were used for special and excursion work north of the border. An example is seen here at Oban on 17 May 1960, waiting to depart with the 6.50pm return to Glasgow. On this occasion, the service had worked outwards with a Fort William portion (detached and joined again at Crianlarich), with steamer connections either way on Loch Linnhe. The outward journey had been via Arrochar, returning via Callander.**
M. Mensing

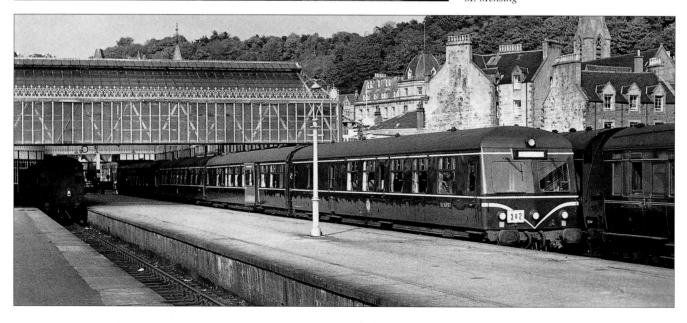

Right: **A close-up of TOPS Class 123 DMBSL No W52086, at Swindon on a trial working on 12 June 1963. The need to include a gangway facility could have resulted in the more usual bland appearance then associated with this type of requirement, although on this occasion a slight modification to the cab windows has resulted in a much bolder and more up-to-date appearance. Pullman-type gangways were fitted throughout.**
A. Swain/Transport Treasury.

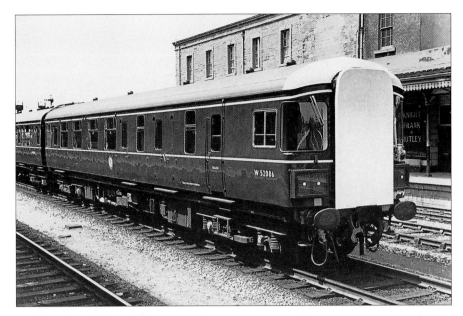

Above: **Passing Netley, between Southampton and Fareham, on 28 October 1966, is a four-coach Class 123 set, led by No W52097. Despite being well liked in service by both crews and passengers alike — the ride was excellent — the buffet cars were withdrawn from service by late 1970 and after that time locomotive-hauled trains began to replace the units on inter-regional workings. This was without doubt a retrograde step, with inferior stock, timings and ride quality, the Portsmouth–Bristol workings for example being either a Class 31 or even on occasions a 'Hampshire' DEMU. Later, one Class 123 buffet car was incorporated into the formation of a Class 309 'Clacton' EMU, replacing an accident-damaged car.**
John H. Bird

Right: **Resplendent in its smart green livery, a long rake of Swindon 'Inter-City' units stands at Taunton on 26 July 1963 with DMSK No W52105 to the fore.** *Carl Symes*

Above: **Coupling compatibility of the sets was Blue Square and as such they could, and on occasions did, run with other units. A combination of old and new 'Inter-City' sets is seen passing Magor on a Bristol to Cardiff semi-fast on 11 August 1963.**
A. J. Wheeler

Left: **Despite their modern appearance and equipment — for instance the latest bogies were fitted, hence the excellent ride — the Swindon sets were destined to be short-lived and most were stored out of service by the mid-1970s. A partial revival occurred later when the entire stock was transferred to the Eastern Region, although again this was to be short term as all had been withdrawn by the summer of 1984. Their former services again reverted to locomotive operation. As a reminder of happier days, a new four-car set is seen on trial at Swindon on 1 February 1963.** *IAL*

Left: **Against a background forest of semaphore arms, a Swindon 'Inter-City' DMU on a Plymouth to Cardiff working arrives at Taunton on 26 July 1963.**
Carl Symes

Above: **With yellow-painted front end, or a yellow plastic blank, an eight-car formation of Swindon units passes Silk Mill Crossing, Taunton, on a Bristol fast, 29 March 1964.** *A. J. Wheeler*

Below: **Pictured at Newport on 10 June 1967, Swindon DMBSL No W52091 is leading its set. There was some suggestion around this time that a conversion to gas turbine propulsion was being considered for one of the units, the work to be undertaken at Derby, but this did not proceed any further than the planning stage.** *A. Swain/Transport Treasury*

Above left: **Passenger accommodation in the Swindon 'Inter-City' sets was of both compartment and open coach layout, of the latest design then available. This is the view of the side corridor on TCL No W59819, recorded new on 19 February 1963.** *BR*

Above right: **The basic Mk 1 concept is readily apparent in the compartment of DMSK No 52097, viewed from the side corridor.** *BR*

Left: **For comparison, here is the interior of Swindon TSL No W59236, also on 19 February 1963. The mirrors were a touch of the old, allied to the new, these being the last coaches built using the oval-design mirrors.** *BR*

Left: **Trailer composite No W59819, again, displaying the corridor side window arrangement. The necessity of having four doors has resulted in an untidy layout not unlike that of the Hawksworth stock built at Swindon not many years earlier. The retention of the old-fashioned slots for carriage numbering, destination boards and conventional buffing gear will also be noted, but modern B4 bogies are fitted.** *J. H. Bird*

Right: **Preceding the 1963 Swindon design were the 'Trans-Pennine' units (TOPS Class 124) of 1960. The similarity is immediately apparent although the sets comprised six vehicles each, with initially one of each type also available as a spare. Power was considerable, with each six-car set able to develop an impressive 1,840hp — necessary indeed when considering some of the fearsome gradients involved in their intended work area. The front end was similar to the contemporary Class 303 EMUs in Scotland, but apparently, the four-digit headcode display was a last-minute addition; it is seen here, hardly used to advantage on a new unit, probably recorded shortly after delivery.** *IAL*

Right: **A Swindon 'Trans-Pennine' set leaves Huddersfield for Leeds with a Metro-Cammell unit alongside. The BR bogies tended to cause the sets to sway somewhat on occasions, allied to a rougher ride at the ends. Knowledgeable passengers would choose their seats carefully.** *P. J. Sharpe*

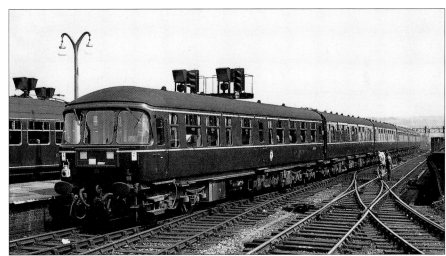

Below: **Leaving Hull on 9 June 1962, a Swindon 'Trans-Pennine' set forms the 3.43pm to Liverpool Lime Street (1M76) while, on the left, Brush Type 2 No D5656 has charge of the 4.30pm to Liverpool Central via Doncaster (1M77).** *I. S. Carr*

Above: **This view of Selby in 1962 shows a secondary 'Trans-Pennine' working awaiting departure. Note the roof board visible on the second carriage**. *P. J. Sharpe*

Below: **By now with characteristic yellow warning panel, a westbound 'Trans-Pennine' DMU is seen nearing Marsden on 17 May 1964.** *J. S. Whiteley*

Left: The buffet, or as it was sometimes referred to, the Griddle Car, of a Swindon 'Trans-Pennine' set. The mural is perhaps a bit unusual — some things from the 1960s are perhaps best forgotten! *IAL*

Below right: Plenty on display by 'Sch . . . — you know who' — to quote the advertising of the period! Food is conspicuous by its absence although, in effect, a reasonably full menu of snack meals was available in the 'Trans-Pennine' Griddle Cars of 1961. *Ian Allan Library*

Above left: As with all buffet vehicles on the railway, the revenue derived from an individual taking his or her time over a solitary drink is hardly cost-effective. BR no doubt wished that patronage would always be as intense as in this posed view of the period, dated 10 February 1966. In keeping with situations elsewhere, the buffet cars were the first casualties, although keeping a drink in the cup on some of the twisting sections of the 'Trans-Pennine' route was an art in itself! *BR*

Right: A first class open saloon of one of the Swindon-built 'Trans-Pennine' trains making a useful comparison in style and apparent expense with previously illustrated DMU interiors. *BR*

Above: **The second build of Scottish-allocated Swindon-built units (Class 126) were identical mechanically to their earlier counterparts (see page 21). To enable them to work with the earlier units, they had the same, by then non-standard, 'White Circle' coupling code. Aside from the obvious livery changes that took place over the years, few major alterations occurred, although the most obvious external variation was the fitting of the then standard four-digit headcode display panel, as seen on DMBSL No Sc51030.** *P. J. Sharpe*

Right: **This is Stranraer Town, the Scottish equivalent of the scene at Pontypool Road seen earlier on page 39, viewed on 17 May 1960. The 12.48pm to Girvan demonstrates the compatibility of the Class 126s with the earlier cars, with No SC51051 leading Nos 79440 and 79088 of the earlier build.** *J. N. Faulkner*

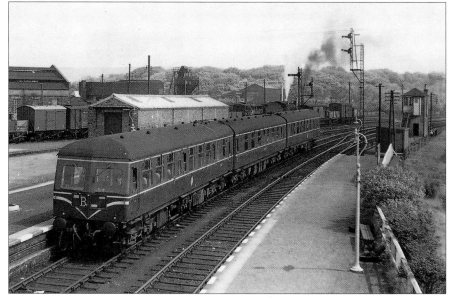

Left: **Another mixed formation, this time with earlier DMBS No SC79082 leading, though the design was common to both batches. The corridor connections which could be used to link sets allowed for two sets facing opposite directions to be coupled together to form a six-car train with ease of access to all facilities for passengers. This was a valiant aim, although it required careful rostering of sets to ensure each unit was always ready and facing in the correct direction, though this was not always possible. Necessity resulted in the aesthetics of the corridor driving end seemingly being of a low priority.** *P. J. Sharpe*

Above: **The neat-looking side of a TFK vehicle makes up a Swindon-built but Scottish Region-allocated set recorded at Kilwinning. All first class seating in the sets was in compartments, with open vehicles used for second class accommodation.** *P. J. Sharpe*

Below: **Concluding the section on the Swindon-built units is this view of a 'reverse' formation depicted at Kilwinning. Such a formation was difficult for both the operators and passengers in one part of the train who would thus be denied access to the buffet facilities, unless prepared to alight and join the correct portion. The leading car is No SC50936.** *P. J. Sharpe*

Upper left: **Birmingham RCW DMBS No M50423 leads the line-up of a three-car set built for use initially on the Crewe–Stoke–Derby service. Introduced from 1957 onwards, these units, allocated TOPS Class 104, were similar to a number built by the Gloucester company. This view was taken in September 1957.** *BR*

Lower left: **In pristine external condition and under the wires at Stockport, a BRCW three-car set leaves for its destination at Manchester.** *P. J. Sharpe*

Upper right: **The first class section of a Birmingham RCW-built unit, which at least afforded pairs of seats with an arm-rest compared with the usual three plus two arrangement for second class. The panelling was wood veneer and at the time this view was taken in 1957 it was uncluttered by the considerable number of warnings and passenger notices that would appear in later years.** *BR*

Centre right: **The interior of a BRCW DMBS saloon, viewed towards the brake compartment. In the immediate foreground is the smoking section, the smaller, non-smoking seating being aft of the vestibule.** *BR*

Below: **One to confuse the modeller! What started off life as a BRCW four-car set here is formed as a three-coach unit with a Metro-Cammell centre coach. The ensemble was depicted at Selby.** *P. J. Sharpe*

Above: **Known as the 'Calder Valley' units due to this being their originally intended area of operation, 30 Birmingham RCW three-car sets were introduced to service from June 1961. Although mechanically similar to other sets with Blue Square compatibility, minor attention to detail in the front-end design resulted in a more pleasing appearance which was in itself similar to the Derby vehicles of 1956. Later TOPS classified as 110, DMCL No E51836 is the leading car.** *BR*

Below: **The trial working of a new Birmingham-built three-car unit is seen arriving at York on 20 June 1961. Today, the scene here is so different: a forest of posts for the overhead wires, track rationalisation and signalling alterations have made it almost unrecognisable.** *S. Creer*

Above: **Views of centre coaches separated from three-car sets are rare; this one, Birmingham TSL No E59695, is depicted at Leeds Neville Hill in 1969. The unusual arrangement of windows either side of the doorways will also be noted and was intended to complement the light and airy interior. Though most of the original centre cars were withdrawn by the end of the 1980s, it is still possible to view a similar sight today as a three-car and a twin-set have survived into preservation.** *D. L. Percival*

Above: **Compare the first class compartment of one of the new 'Calder Valley' Birmingham three-car units with its two-aside seating, with the three plus two second class seating visible in the distance.** *BR*

Above: **The driver's control desk of a Birmingham DMCL as built. The Rolls-Royce plate will be noted.** *IAL*

Right: **From its appearance, Birmingham RCW DMCL No E51829 had not long been in service when recorded at Middlesbrough circa 1961/2. The aluminium surrounds to the windows would later be painted over, although, in the opinion of many, it was this original styling that displayed the units to their best advantage.** *P. J. Sharpe*

Below: **Within a few years of entering service, yellow panels had been added to the ends of the 'Calder Valley' sets, although when this photograph was taken both the route indicator and destination blind remained in use. A six-car formation of two three-coach sets is seen leaving Hebden Bridge with the 10.30am Liverpool Exchange to Harrogate via Bradford and Leeds service on 14 October 1963.** *D. Ian Wood*

Above: **A BRCW Class 118, later-type three-car set including a composite centre vehicle is seen here at Dawlish while running on the 3.5pm Exeter St Davids to Kingswear working in late June 1960.** *M. Mensing*

Below: **The Millbay branch in Plymouth sees an empty Birmingham RCW set passing Belmont Sidings on the left and Harwell Street sidings to the right, on 28 August 1961.** *R. C. Riley/Transport Treasury*

Above: **The firm of Cravens, originally the Cravens Railway Carriage & Wagon Company, was responsible for three similar design railcars: two multiple-units for passenger service and a single-car type for parcels. They were introduced between 1956 and 1959, with the passenger units originally formed as either two- or three-car sets. Dating from 1959, the Rolls-Royce-powered units were fitted with hydraulic transmission and torque converters and proved unreliable in service; consequently this series was extinct as early as 1969. They were allocated TOPS Class 113.**

The two- and three-car Cravens-built units were very much a hybrid of different design styles and fittings with BR Mk 1 standard coach windows, doors and sundry interior fittings allied to what was basically bus-type seating. Externally the front-end design afforded the usual excellent forward vision, although the limited number of access doors created problems when they were used on suburban routes, where rapid access and egress were a prerequisite. An example of this problem was the batch which was originally intended for use on the Midland & Great Northern route but was sent instead to King's Cross when the M&GN line closed in 1959. Seen brand-new in 1956, DMBS No E50359 is leading what would later be deemed as Class 105. *IAL*

Centre left: **The interior layout of a Cravens driving trailer, seen in 1983, portraying the bus-type seating to advantage. A number of TSL and TCL vehicles were also built to make some of the sets up to three cars, but these were all deemed surplus to requirements as early as 1970 and were withdrawn.** *J. G. Glover*

Left: **A works view of a power bogie from a Cravens unit in 1957. The extensions to the buffer stocks will be noted as will the then standard means of connecting DMUs with a conventional screw coupling.** *Cravens Ltd*

Right: **Two identical Cravens sets have just passed each other near Croft, Leicestershire, on 21 September 1961. The nearest train is the 11.10am Nuneaton (Trent Valley) to Leicester London Road, while in the distance is the 11.10 ex-Leicester.** *M. Mensing*

Below: **A three-car Cravens-built set arrives at Trent on a Derby train in April 1962. Externally similar to the later Class 112 type units, the Class 105 cars numbered in the M50752-817 series had mechanical transmission although both types were of the Blue Square coupling code. Livery is in the interim stage with green bodywork, whiskers and electric warning flashes, the next step being half yellow ends, after which would come the bland corporate styling of full yellow ends and blue bodywork.** *A. J. Wheeler*

Right: **Cravens DMCL No 51720 heads a six-car train passing through Colne. In the number series 51681–51730, these units were later briefly designated Class 112 before withdrawal from traffic.** *P. J. Sharpe*

Above: **The advantage of coupling compatibility is well demonstrated again, as a two-car Gloucester RCW unit (TOPS Class 100) leads a three-car Metro-Cammell set east of Humber Road Junction, Coventry, on the 1.25pm Birmingham New Street to Rugby working on 9 November 1963.** *M. Mensing*

Centre left: **Another mixed formation working as a Metropolitan-Cammell twin-set leads a Gloucester twin, still with the ubiquitous steam-age tail-lamp, through Princes Street Gardens en route for North Berwick.** *P. J. Sharpe*

Lower left: **In service on the Scottish Region, a Gloucester two-car set in the Sc56300-19 series arrives at Polmont with the 1.55pm service from Falkirk (Grahamston) on 1 September 1961. The guard again perhaps a little hasty in his bid to leave his unit!** *S. Rickard*

Right: **New and seemingly on crew familiarisation/training duty, Gloucester DMSL No W51106 was photographed late in 1959. It sports a frontal design very similar to Derby-built units. These sets were allocated TOPS Class 119.** *P. J. Sharpe*

Below: **Also brand-new and posed for the photographer, stands a Gloucester three-car set with DMBC No W51056 leading. The motor brake composite had seating for 18 first class and 16 second class passengers.** *P. J. Sharpe*

Bottom: **The same three-car set is here seen in service with its trailer buffet second and with a Mk 1 full brake attached at the rear. The combination was recorded near to Over Junction, Gloucester.** *P. J. Sharpe*

Left: **A front-end study at Birmingham Moor Street on 13 January 1962. This Gloucester set had just been given the yellow-end treatment.** *M. Mensing*

Below: **Another mixed combination again displays to advantage the benefit of compatible coupling codes. A three-car Gloucester unit is attached to a three-car Swindon 'Cross-country' set on the 5.5pm Birmingham Snow Hill to Swansea service at Acocks Green on 22 April 1959.** *M. Mensing*

Above: **This view shows a Gloucester three-car unit which has had the centre vehicle temporarily removed.** *IAL*

Centre right: **A view of the opposite side of a TSLRB vehicle — No W59424. This one has had its catering facilities removed. Notice also the Hawksworth-designed vehicle coupled next to it on the right.**
P. J. Sharpe

Lower right: **This photograph shows a three-car Gloucester unit with a green-painted Hawksworth corridor vehicle inserted in the middle, which is 'through-wired' as necessary. Hawksworth coaches were converted for this purpose at Swindon to upgrade three-car units to four cars when required. The whole ensemble is attached to a three-car Swindon 'Cross-country' unit. The combination is forming the 3.45pm Oxford to Paddington and was recorded just after leaving Didcot on 22 September 1961.** *M. Mensing*

Left: Two designs of single-unit bogie vehicle, later TOPS Classes 121 and 122, were operated by BR from 1960 and 1958 respectively. Externally they were similar, although the 1958-built vehicles of Class 122, constructed by the Gloucester Railway Carriage & Wagon Company, were marginally lighter at 35 tons than the 37 tons of the Pressed Steel Company vehicles. No W55000, the first of the Gloucester batch, is seen when brand-new outside Swindon stock shed on 4 May 1958. *A. Swain/Transport Treasury*

Right: This view of the other end of a single car shows a Gloucester unit in the picturesque setting of the south Devon hills. No W55000 leaves Dainton Tunnel with the 4.28pm Newton Abbot to Kingsbridge service on 23 September 1961. *W. L. Underhay*

Left: Brand-new Gloucester unit No W55001 was recorded on 1 May 1958, just prior to entering service on the Western Region. Note the exhaust pipes carried over the driving end. *P. J. Sharpe*

Right: Intended for use initially on both the Western and London Midland regions, the single units, or 'bubble cars' as they were later known by enthusiasts, were coupling compatible and saw operation on a variety of lightly used services. The intention was for them to reduce operating costs, and while this was certainly the case, they did not always mean that a previously loss-making working became profitable. No W55009 was recorded at Stratford-upon-Avon. *P. J. Sharpe*

Right: **Gloucester No W55015 waits in the peaceful setting of Looe, ready to return to Liskeard with the 11.1am service on 1 May 1964. This car was converted for parcels use in 1968 as a DMLV, in which form it became Class 131.** *M. York*

Right: **The single units were also ideal for servicing the lightly patronised stations on main line routes, although here their presence did not always lead to the retention of such workings. A Gloucester unit is seen at Aynho Junction on the 4.2pm stopping, Princes Risborough to Banbury local on 29 August 1962.** *M. Mensing*

Right: **A line on which the introduction of single-car units failed to afford sufficient increase of traffic was the Brent to Kingsbridge branch in Devon. A Gloucester unit approaches the summit of the climb out of the terminus on its way to Brent on 12 August 1961.** *R. E. Toop*

Above: **A pair of Gloucester units with two milk tanks in tow crosses the Royal Albert Bridge with the then new road bridge alongside, while, underneath, the route of the former Southern line is visible. This was one of the rare occasions when two items of tail traffic were attached to a diesel service. The formation is seen on the eastern end of Brunel's famous bridge, heading for Plymouth on 29 April 1962.** *Brian Haresnape*

Left: **As well as the single-car units, the build from each manufacturer (20 Gloucester and 16 Pressed Steel), included a further batch of unpowered driving trailers (nine Gloucester and 10 Pressed Steel), these weighing 29 tons each. This allowed flexibility of operation by increasing accommodation as required as the two BUT (AEC) 150hp engines of each power car were well able to cope with the additional load. No W55007 and a DTS arrive at Hatton with the 6.45pm Stratford-upon-Avon to Leamington Spa service on 2 July 1960.** *M. Mensing*

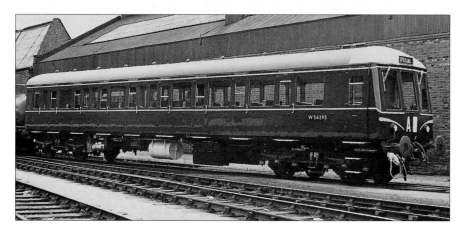

Left: **One of the associated driving trailer second cars, No W56295, is being shunted by a fireless locomotive when brand-new at Gloucester's works. These cars almost invariably ran as required with the single cars in the W55000 series.** *P. J. Sharpe*

Upper right: **With DTS No W56299 leading, this Gloucester two-car set is seen near Hatton. From the passenger's perspective, the introduction of this type of diesel car allowed for a hitherto unfamiliar view of the route ahead and was an undoubted success. Less popular though was the ponderous and laborious gear change and transmission noises so associated with this and several other contemporary types of DMU.** *P. J. Sharpe*

Right: **Gloucester DMBS No W55016 with a DTS is seen at Southall on 9 May 1959.** *J. C. Haydon*

Below: **Following their introduction on the Western Region (WR) in 1958, the single units quickly spread to most areas of the system, so ousting steam on a number of suburban workings. Indeed, by as early as June 1958, the Stratford to Leamington services was reported as almost entirely in the hands of these vehicles. A pair of Gloucester-built cars with No W55004 leading, descends Hatton Bank on one such working, the 6.45 Stratford-upon-Avon to Leamington Spa on 14 June 1958.** *M. Mensing*

Above: **Ten motor luggage vans of Class 128 were delivered from the Gloucester Railway Carriage & Wagon Co in early 1960 for use on the London Midland and Western regions. The six for service on the WR had end gangways fitted as standard. Powered by two 230hp engines per vehicle, they were well able to accommodate a trailing load when required. DMPV No M55987 is seen when brand-new.** *IAL*

Left: **As a comparison to the previous picture, this is one of the WR-allocated parcels vehicles, No W55995, seen on an evening working approaching Knowle & Dorridge on the Birmingham–Leamington Spa main line on 10 June 1960.** *M. Mensing*

Lower left: **In pristine external condition, DMPV No W55993 is at work in the London suburbs circa 1960.** *R. C. Riley/ Transport Treasury*

Upper right: **Changing traffic patterns rendered the LMR-allocated vehicles redundant in 1982 and they were withdrawn. Five of the six WR cars survived until 1990, although by then minus any trace of a gangway and having also undergone several livery/sector colour schemes. No W55992 is seen on a down working passing Spring Road on the North Warwickshire line near Birmingham on 29 September 1960.** *M. Mensing*

Lower right: **This train comprises just a single parcels railcar and one van. No W55995 heads north at Worcester on Sunday, 27 August 1961.** *M. Mensing*

Upper left: **Possibly one the best known of all DMU types — no doubt because of the number and longevity of vehicles built — the Metropolitan-Cammell units were introduced as three separate series in 1955, 1956 and 1957. The 1955-type units were 'Lightweights' and consisted of 36 two-car sets. These were unique, compared with the later-build Metro-Cammell units, having a Yellow Diamond coupling code (see pages 19, 20). With the closure of many lines on which they had originally worked they were destined for an early demise, all having gone by 1969. The initial build was followed by no fewer than 637 vehicles of the same external appearance, this time made up of two-, three- and four-car sets, mostly of Class 101.**

Metro-Cammell DMCL No M50322 (1956 series, built in 1958) leads a three-car set waiting to leave Birmingham New Street for Leicester with the 5.10pm on 15 April 1958. This was the day after steam had relinquished its role on the Leicester-Burton-Nottingham-Birmingham services. Standing on the left is Class 4 2-6-0 No 43049. This car remained in service until 2000 and a number of the sets remained in regular service until 2003; indeed, some still survive in departmental use in 2004.
M. Mensing

Lower left: **With crews still in the characteristic steam uniform, a two-car Metro-Cammell set waits to leave Birmingham New Street on the 4.20pm to Redditch on 17 September 1960. Alongside is 'Crab' 2-6-0 No 42859.** *M. Mensing*

Above: **Metro-Cammell DMBS No M50312 leads a three-car set with centre car TCL No M59123, at Stafford.** *IAL*

Below: **The original second class seating in this Metro-Cammell car was in green, offset by light green Formica panelling.**
Kenneth Field

Above: **Caught while paused between services are two three-car sets of the 1957 Metro-Cammell stock with Rolls-Royce engines, designated Class 111, Nos E50275, E59105, E50285 and E50276, E59106, E50286.** *Kenneth Field*

Centre left: **The sump side of the Rolls-Royce 180hp engine of a Metro-Cammell Class 111 DMCL. To the left is the clutch housing.** *Kenneth Field*

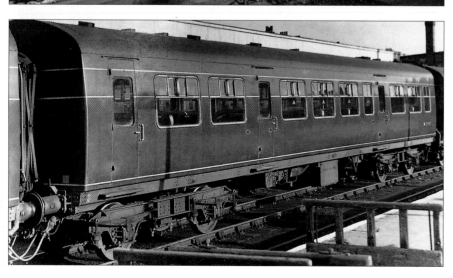

Lower left: **The centre coach of a Metro-Cammell unit is shown, complete with the original type of scissors gangway connections. This is TSL No NE59109, seen at Doncaster on 10 April 1965.** *D. L. Percival*

Right: **With 1970s fashions in evidence, this is the first class section of prototype refurbished Metro-Cammell DMCL No 51518. Compare this with the original decor shown on page 71.** *IAL*

Below: **An unusual combination of a Metro-Cammell power car, No M50136, coupled to LMS dynamometer car No 3 and an unidentified second coach, is recorded during a brief stopover at Skipton whilst on trial on 19 September 1957. As built, the vehicles in this series, Class 111 Nos M50134-7, had two Rolls-Royce 180hp engines, although it was reported that this particular car had been temporarily fitted with two supercharged engines each of 230hp. Whether any useful advantage was gained from the revised equipment is not known although suffice to say there is no record of such power plants being fitted to others of the type.** *N. Shelley*

Upper left: **The Park Royal company built 20 two-car units for BR from November 1957 and so continued a tradition of DMU building that had commenced with the GWR some years earlier. Similar, although not identical, in appearance to some of the Derby units, the London-built vehicles had a riveted body which tended to work loose over the years, leading to a number of complaints from both crews and passengers. Only one vehicle of each set was powered, which could result in the single power car struggling under certain circumstances. No M56156, a DTCL, is seen at Walsall on 4 May 1958.** *P. J. Sharpe*

Above: **An official view of the undergear of Park Royal DMBS No M50397 recorded at its works on 6 March 1958.** *Park Royal Vehicles Ltd*

Below: **The interior of a non-powered Park Royal trailer, displaying the bright fabric originally used for the seating. In a two-car unit, accommodation was for a total of 116 passengers including 16 in first class.** *Park Royal Vehicles Ltd*

Lower left: **A two-coach Park Royal unit in service at Bescot leaves the station on the 4.10pm Birmingham New Street to Rugeley working on 17 March 1962.** *M. Mensing*

Left: Pressed Steel DMBS No W51332 at Southall in what appears to be brand-new condition. The date is likely to have been at the end of 1959 when this, the first of the TOPS Class 117 units, was delivered. *P. J. Sharpe*

Right: A Pressed Steel three-car suburban unit at Fleet on a Basingstoke to Waterloo service, circa 1965. This was an unusual working as this service was well known for still being steam-hauled at that time. *A. D. McIntyre*

Left: Away from its more usual Western Region haunts, this Pressed Steel three-car set runs into Southampton Terminus with the 5.10pm from Reading on 8 May 1961 with DMBS No W51374 leading. At this time, the majority of through workings from the WR to Southampton were still steam hauled so this was a somewhat unusual sight for the period. *J. C. Haydon*

Left: With its characteristic rectangular buffers, a Pressed Steel three-car unit negotiates what was then still referred to as Kingham Junction, on 2 September 1961, with the 5.37pm from Oxford. *M. Mensing*

Right: **When brand-new, on 24 August 1960, a Pressed Steel unit waits at Oxford on a wet summer's day, having arrived from Swindon.** *B. H. Jackson*

Below left: **The interior of a Pressed Steel suburban set from the Western Region, photographed officially on 1 August 1963. Again, Formica has been used to a great degree while the end-of-seat grab handles were a useful, if at times painful, addition.** *BR*

Below right: **The centre cars were these 63ft 10in composite vehicles, with seats for 24 first class and 50 second. This example, TCL No W59487, by then in blue livery, was seen at Oxford on 16 October 1976.** *Brian Morrison*

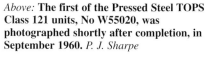

Above: **The first of the Pressed Steel TOPS Class 121 units, No W55020, was photographed shortly after completion, in September 1960.** *P. J. Sharpe*

Right: **A scene that would later be consigned to history — the coal concentration yard. This one was at Thorney Road near West Drayton, as a single unit passes on the West Drayton to Staines West service on 12 October 1963.** *T. Wright*

Left: **Another view of Pressed Steel No W55020, possibly at a similar time to the previous view. Square buffers were fitted to the units when new and the livery was of course all-over green with yellow/orange 'whiskers' and white ends to the roof above the cab.** *P. J. Sharpe*

Left: **A Class 121 unit waits at Slough with the shuttle service to Windsor on 23 December 1961.** *IAL*

Right: **The tail traffic attached to Pressed Steel DMBS No W55022 is in the form of an LMS full brake; the train being recorded near Saunderton on 29 August 1961 was the 3.6pm Maidenhead to Aylesbury working.** *H. Harman*

Above: **DMBS No E50415, the power car of a Wickham unit, is portrayed when brand-new. Later designated Class 109, these units were introduced in 1957. Still to be added are the 'whiskers', while the white tyres would not last long in service.** *IAL*

Left: **Just five two-car units were produced by Wickham in Hertfordshire and, of these, two complete sets were withdrawn for sale to Trinidad Railways as early as 1961. Leading this four-coach set at King's Lynn is one of these, DMBS No E50419. Another set, Nos E50416 and E56171, spent over 25 years in Departmental stock, mostly as a General Manager's Saloon, and is now preserved.** *IAL*

Cover captions:

Front: **The driver of Gloucester RCW single power car No. W55013 collects the token from the signalman at Bromyard Junction, Worcester on a warm summer's day in 1963, prior to taking the single line to Bromyard.** *Michael Mensing*

Rear top: **A freshly-repainted Derby Lightweight is pictured near Penrith in the summer of 1965 having just started its scenic journey theough the Lake District to Keswick. The line beyond there to Cockermouth and Workington closed the following spring, but the Penrith-Keswick section survived until 1972.** *Michael Mensing*

Rear middle: **An almost-new Swindon Cross-Country unit, later classified Class 120, enters Glasgow Queen Street station in 1961. The superb semaphore signal gantry is but a distant memory now.** *Michael Mensing*

Rear bottom: **One of the last Metro-Cammell two-car sets to be built, led by DTCL No SC56405, runs over the level crossing at Park on the Ballater branch in 1964.** *Michael Mensing*